God's Plan
for
Children

The Church's responsibility
to the next generation

by
DAVE ROBERTS

EASTBOURNE

ISBN 1 84291 122 8

Published by Kingsway Communications
Lottbridge Drove, Eastbourne, East Sussex BN23 6NT, England.
Email: childrensministry@kingsway.co.uk

Cover design and print production for the publishers by
Bookprint Creative Services, PO Box 827, BN21 3YJ, England.
Printed in Great Britain

For Ben and Joel.
Thanks for all you've taught me.

Contents

Introduction

Hope is a precious gift. Daring to hope is a vital choice that parents, people and churches must make as we face the uncertainties of a new millennium.

It would be easy to be overwhelmed by a counsel of despair from the massed choirs of advisers, experts and media commentators, who reflect on society and our children.

There is, it seems, a creeping inevitability about the decline of children attending church, growing crime rates among juveniles, the disturbances of the disrupted child, alienated by his or her broken home, the hyper-competitive nature of the playground clique and the relentless pressure of media dispensed visions of what it is to be fashionable.

Do we dare to say that a nation of children can be called back to the knowledge of a loving Father, the earthy human realities found in the life and work of his Son and the present day empowerment of the Holy Spirit?

Would we allow a mustard seed of faith to grow in our hearts that would grow into a belief that a nation can be transformed? It will, if we will have the patience to invest relentlessly, persistently and lovingly into the lives of a generation quite literally lost, with no map to guide them back to belief, hope and a relationship with God.

If our hope is to be more than a heroic yearning, fading painfully into disappointment, we must have our own map or guidebook to the future of ministry to children.

As a parent, church leader and someone who works with children and children's workers, I need reference points, an underlying framework that will shape my thinking, vision and the plan that flow from them.

This book is built on one such framework, a seven-point declaration of intent. It's not a closed set of principles. We may have more to discover as the wisdom gained from everyday experiences accrues. But it's a place to start.

Dave Roberts, Eastbourne, November 2002

A Declaration of Intent

There are seven practical ways that the church can seek to ensure that the good news of Jesus reaches a new generation of children. As we begin this exploration of hope, here are some defining statements that could guide us towards the re-evangelisation of our nation and the transformation of society.

We recognise that the privilege of calling a generation to Jesus is part of our life task, and a role of all involved in the Church.

We therefore commit to:

Making our work with children a priority.
We recognise that there will be many ways of reaching children and nurturing them in the Christian faith. We commit to helping provide significant finance, resources and a call for people to carry out the tasks.

Equipping Christian parents to affirm, discipline and nurture their children.
Knowing that many will feel helpless in the face of contemporary culture and beliefs, we will offer both biblical insight and practical ideas to help parents tell the story of Jesus, celebrate their relationship with God, introduce children to prayer, and offer wise words in the everyday conversations that help plant the seeds of truth.

Being deliberate in our plans and strategies to reach children outside of church life.
We believe that we can bless children by providing opportunities for relaxation, challenge and social interaction. Using many different formats and styles, we will seek in our words and our deeds to 'build a bridge' for truth into their lives.

Grasping the opportunity to participate in the education of children.
Just as Jesus and his contemporaries learnt practical knowledge and eternal truth at the synagogue school in Nazareth, we understand that we have an opportunity to tell the Christian story and speak of Christian values through the school system. Through our own resources, and in coalition with other like-minded churches, we commit to helping every child, in every school in our locality, to hear the Good News of Jesus several times during their formal education.

Calling the Church to action
Committed as we are to our neighbourhood we will use our influence to promote the vital task of reaching children to the wider church. Where our church influences a

denomination, a Bible College, or any other group that seeks to give direction to church life, we will – with a mixture of boldness and grace – call for an adoption of the central tenets of this declaration as a key part of the strategy and curriculum that they offer.

Providing culture that uplifts

We will intentionally seek out and promote to our children, (via home and church) music, reading and other cultural expressions of a Biblical faith. We will by this means impart a sense of wonder; a God centred way of seeing and a joy in believing. We do this as a response to the theft of their innocence by some aspects of mass media culture. We will also seek to help our children discern popular culture, recognising and responding to that which seeks for truth, and rejecting that which celebrates evil or deception.

Being world Christians with a heart for children

We will affirm and encourage those people who call out for justice, compassion and protection of children in need around the world.

Imagine what a tenderhearted generation could do!

1. Why the church must make children a priority

We recognise that there will be many ways of reaching children and nurturing them in the Christian faith. We commit to helping provide significant finance, resources and a call for people to carry out the tasks.

Why the church must make children a priority
It is my belief that there will be a spiritual revival in many nations of the world during the coming decades.

There will be multiple reasons for this. Worldwide prayer movements will release a passion for evangelism; Adults will be won by the reflective, process of faith discovery found in courses such as Alpha; World events will prompt a renewed sense of spiritual need; Individual Christians will carry their faith to the communities in which they live.

But a key factor will be a renewed purpose in the worldwide church with respect to children.

The need is urgent. A church leader from Liverpool, England told me that youth work in his area is often futile. 'They are hardened criminals by the age of 12,' he said, 'If we don't reach them before that they become difficult to speak to.' He has put his words into action and is part of a team that reaches over 2,000 unchurched children every week.

His passion is needed. The 1999 UK church survey conducted by Christian Research told us that the 'tide is going out', and warned that children attending church on Sunday had dropped from 14% to 8% in the United Kingdom, in just one decade (1989-1999).

The challenge for the church is this:

Are we prepared to put the same strategic, financial and people resources into nurturing the children of the church, and reaching the unchurched child, that we pour into our evangelism courses, youth work and church fabric budgets?

Are we willing via schools work, midweek clubs, Sunday schools and specialist programmes, to 're-stock' our society with the knowledge of the Christian story?

Will we seek to create a climate where a seed planted in the life of a child can bear fruit in the teenage or adults years? Will we make this a priority?

Gavin Reid, the former Bishop of Maidstone believes we must. He told a gathering of children's evangelists that research indicated that '76% of adult converts refer to childhood faith experiences'.

These then are the headlines. How can we begin to implement these goals? First we need to clarify the principles that will inform our actions.

From a firm foundation

Much of the way we think is expressed in proverbs or short verses. We all need memorable lines that capture our understanding of life and how to live it.

When you think of children, verses such as: 'Train up a

child in the way that they should go and when they are old they will not depart from it' (Proverbs 22:6), and 'suffer the little children to come unto me' (Matthew 19:14) spring immediately to mind.

Behind these pithy proverbs, however, lies a pattern of thought in the Bible that can help us understand our roots. From these roots spring our values. From these values spring our actions. Before we can discover God's plan for the children of this generation, we must first discern his eternal heart for children.

His Heart

There are six distinct biblical patterns that will guide us as we seek to work with children. These are:

• God loves and values children from their conception.

• God asks parents to both teach and care for their children, and gives the parent the primary role in their spiritual nurture.

• Children are to be involved in our communal worship gatherings.

• God uses children and youth at pivot points in the salvation history of Israel as his messengers. The Bible values age and wisdom for government and authority, but clearly mandates children to be carriers of truth into the most difficult of situations.

• Jesus was very clear cut in including children when others were ready to exclude or marginalise them.

• The Scripture returns again and again to a concern for the orphan and widowed, and also has significant counsel for parents regarding the physical and emotional well being of their children.

We will also find it rewarding if we seek an understanding of education in Bible times. All of the above combine to give us a comprehensive picture. Let's look now at the details.

God's heart for children
The Psalms are a rich source of insight into God's heart for children. Psalm 71:6 reminds us that 'From my birth I have relied on you, you brought me forth from my mother's womb. I will ever praise you.'

The Christian concern for the child is rooted in the recognition that we are all made in the image of God (Genesis 1:26), and that each and every child has dignity and purpose as a result.

The psalmist in Psalm 139:13-14 tells us that God has 'Created my inmost being; you knit me together in my mother's womb. I praise you because I am fearfully and wonderfully made.'

As you read on you will discover a rich matrix of biblical teaching on nurture, discipline and the passing on of the faith. The foundation of it all, however, is that we worship a God whose 'loving kindess endureth forever' (Psalm 136) and who is 'slow to anger and abounding in mercy… as a father has compassion on his children, so the Lord has compassion on those who fear him' (Psalm 103).

We need to help our children grasp the compassion of their heavenly father. As we start on a journey of understanding about work with children, it's the release of a 'sense of wonder'; an awe, a reverence and an amazement that we want to enable, with the help of the Holy Spirit, to enter their lives. Telling stories and drawing the conclusions is not enough, unless they feel the heartbeat of the Father of creation through all we say and do.

An understanding of the grace that God shows towards us and the godly joy that can be our response is vital. The authors of *The Child in Christian Thought* (Eerdmans) describe the attitude towards children of the key figures of the last 2,000 years. All, it seemed, were trying to walk the tightrope between discipline and nurture. Some emphasised the sinfulness and rebellion of the child and the need for strong discipline.

Others, such as the early church father John Chrysostom, believed that our rebellion 'soiled' the image of God within us, rather than causing us to be 'totally depraved'. God, in this view, has taken the initiative to heal and restore us through the life, death and resurrection of Jesus.

Chrysostom used the metaphor of the artist as a description of parents.

'To each of you fathers and mothers, I say, just as we see artists fashioning their paintings and statues with great precision, so we must care for these wondrous statues of ours. Painters, when they have set the canvas on the easel paint on it day by day to accomplish their purpose.'

Gregory and Suzanne Wolfe writing in *Circle of Grace* (Ballantine) capture it beautifully:

'The secret to your child's moral and spiritual development is this: Your child should not simply admire goodness, but should actually fall in love with goodness.'

17

The theologian, Horace Bushnell, writing in his landmark *Christian Nurture* expresses it this way:

> 'We should rather seek to teach a feeling than a doctrine; to bathe the child in their own feeling of love of God and dependence on Him...; to make what is good, happy and attractive, what is wrong, odious and hateful; then as understanding advances, to give it food suited to its capacity.'

This emphasis on the grace of God through Jesus as the dominant note in the biblical symphony creates a different response than a theological tune dominated by God's judgement of rebellious, hard-hearted people. The second view is important, but is by no means the only theme in the Scripture. It the warning note to those inclined to take God's love for granted.

Extensive research, with over 8,000 individuals, by the Lutheran sponsored Search Institute identified 10 characteristics of committed youth. Understanding grace and living in grace is considered key. The authors reflect in *Passing on the Faith* (St Mary's Press) that:

> 'If a grace-oriented relationship with God is not modelled and taught... the tendency of children and youth is to interpret Christianity as a religion of expectations, demands or requirements. As a result, many grow into adulthood assuming that their efforts to live a good life qualify them as Christians. Their attention is on what they do and not on what God has done, is doing and will do for them.'

On the frontline of grace

Another major thread in the faith and life tapestry is the role of the parent. The church fathers have been very clear on this. The parent or influential adult is a key 'means of grace' for the child. Martin Luther said 'Most certainly father and mother are apostles, bishops and priests to their children, for it is they who make them acquainted with the gospel.' Karl Barth encourages parents to 'joyfully invite children to "rejoice" with them in God.'

The parent has the potential to interact with the child in several ways. We shall deal with these in greater depth in the next chapter, but include a summary here.

• **Facts** – the parent shares the facts of the faith.

• **Example** – the parent offers the child an example of Christ.

• **Revelation** – the parent equips the child for revelation by introducing them to the Scripture and prayer.

• **Doing** – the parent helps the child 'learn by doing'.

• **Parable** – the parent shares their own faith and that of others via story telling.

• **Tradition** – the parent promotes everyday rituals and traditions that provide both order, structure and faith content for the child.

• **Reference** - the parent is an anchor and a reference point for the child as they learn the lessons of life.

This ideal is not always the reality. In *Passing on the Faith* the authors tell us that their research indicates that the average church going family is not talking about faith to their children (65% reported no family devotional life). Walter Brueggemann, theologian and writer notes that:

> 'One major function of intergenerational life is to transmit the stories and promises which identify the family, so that each new generation has an inheritance that gives both identity and roots, purpose and vocation.'

Much of this happens in the mundane things of life. The National Merit Scholars organisation found that the one thing that most of the high achieving students had in common was that they ate dinner with their family almost every day. The key factor in their growth was domestic.

Christian thinkers from across the traditions and from around the world, are calling the church to rediscover the primacy of the 'domestic church'. In the face of societal breakdown and the spiritually thin Christian household it may seem like a new message, but it's timeless, echoing through the Scripture and church history.

The influential thinker and theologian Jonathan Edwards reminds us:

> 'Every Christian family ought to be as it were a little church consecrated to Christ… family education and order are some of the chief means of grace. If these fail all other means are likely to prove ineffectual.'

This positive influence is not solely the prerogative of the traditional two-parent family, with positive adults and circles of adult acquaintance also being crucial for a child's growth and maturity. A University of California study into why some teens from difficult situations were more resilient than others discovered that:

'They all experienced the non-exploitative interest, care and support of at least one adult during their childhood years – a parent or grandparent, aunt or uncle, older brother or sister, coach or teacher, pastor or youth leader.'

We will dwell in more depth in the next chapter on biblical wisdom for parents and adults. Suffice it to say, their role is key.

The gathered church
The family may be the 'hot house' of Christian growth, but the role of the wider church is also important and vital. The Jewish experience of faith was intergenerational, and found particular expression in feasts and celebrations.

Moses told the people of Israel: 'Assemble the people – men, women and children, and the aliens living in your towns – so they can listen and learn to fear the Lord your God and follow carefully all the words of this law' (Deuteronomy 31:12-13).

The people gathered with their children to hear Jehosaphat and the prophecy of Jahaziel (2 Chronicles 20:13). In the book of Joel God urges the people to gather for a solemn assembly. 'Bring together the elders, gather the children, those nursing at the breast' (Joel 2).

Water Brueggemann reminds us that the liturgies, ceremonies and practices of our churches are part of the child's mental landscape. He talks of 'defining memories' and how the church remembers its roots and children perceive these ceremonies of remembrance.

He cites five key biblical incidents, occurrences or traditions.

• **The Passover Feast** – a special meal remembering the deliverance of Israel from Egypt (Exodus 12).

• **The Feast of Unleavened Bread** – a seven day feast which involved a special diet (Exodus 13:8).

• **The Offer of the Firstborn** – the first child was to be 'given over to the Lord', as was the firstborn of all the animals a family owned (Exodus 13:14).

• **The Ten Commandments** – these and other decrees and stipulations guided the people in their new found freedom (Deuteronomy 5 & 6).

• **Crossing the Jordan** – this was followed by a special ceremony where symbolic stories created a memorial to God's provision (Joshua 4).

Running through the biblical accounts is a reminder that these communal celebrations and actions will provoke the curiosity of children. All the passages remind the fathers and mothers to be ready to respond to the questions of a child about the ceremonies, with the stories behind the symbolic acts. They are stories of deliverance and God's provision. Israel being spared God's judgement; Israel being delivered from the hands of the Egyptians; Israel crossing the Jordan on dry ground when it should have been in flood.

These seemingly odd acts or rituals speak of the root memories and root values of the people, although on the surface they seem non-rational. The world, the child learns, is not as it seems.

The gathered church meeting, it would appear, is a time to remember and re-enact the deliverance that God has bought us through Christ's life, death and resurrection. The parent in this situation helps the child grasp the history behind the liturgy, ceremony and song. The role of festivals such as Christmas, Easter and the Bible Weeks that many attend mirrors the Old Testament celebration of salvation history.

Mark DeVries, writing in *Family Based Youth Ministry* (IVP) notes the findings of the United Church of Australia regarding the involvement of children and youth in the congregational worship life of the church:

> 'The researchers discovered that people who grew up in church attending worship but not Sunday school were much more likely to be involved in church as adults than were young people who had only attended the Sunday school without attending the worship.'

Whatever arrangements we make for the formal teaching of our children in a church context, it seems clear that there is an important role for the multigenerational congregation celebrating the goodness of God together.

God uses children
Neither are children mere spectators in the drama of salvation history. We will examine their role in more depth in another chapter, but let's consider the following at this point:

• **Daniel and his friends** – defied their persecutors, even to the point of death.

• **Samuel** – heard from God, prophesied to the chief priest.

• **Josiah** – raised to reverence God, acted swiftly against pagan idolatry.

- **Naaman's maid** – gave the advice that led to his healing.

- **David** – challenged Goliath, the man the nation feared.

- **Jeremiah** – told not to use his youth as an excuse.

- **Joseph** – his ability to interpret dreams caused him great pain, but was to lead to greatness.

- **Jesus** – debated with the High Priest at the age of twelve.

- **Mary** – a teenage girl who gave birth to the Messiah.

The biblical record and a wide range of commentaries suggest that all of the above were either children or teenagers.

Are we ready to give children and teenagers tasks within the life of the church? Are we willing to admit to the possibility that they might have insights and perceptions prompted by the Holy Spirit that are every bit as valid as the pastor, the vicar, the deacon, the elder or the PCC member?

Jesus certainly thought so.

Jesus and Children

Jesus' attitude to children is deeply instructive. He drew them in from the fringes, but also made it clear that despite the high regard of his culture and the scriptures for the family, following him took precedence.

In Mark 10:13-16 we read of Jesus calling the children to him. He was indignant at the disciples attempt to exclude them. The disciples reflected the culture of the day, which didn't encourage women or children to participate in the

24

more formal teaching and discussion that surrounded rabbinic figures like Jesus.

Jesus makes his point strongly by insisting that 'The Kingdom of heaven belongs to such as these'. His audience would have expected a kingdom and a Messiah that would free them from the burden of the Romans. Jesus places children at the centre of his kingdom.

Jesus also held children up as an example to adults: 'Unless you become as a child' (Mark 10:15) reminds his listeners that the uncynical trust of a child is an example to them, but also clearly infers the child's ability to have a personal relationship with God.

Jesus goes on to warn adults that they are not to lead children into sin or they will face a severe judgement. In a poignant and powerful statement he reminds the adults to have the humility of a child and to be aware that when they welcome a child they welcome Jesus (Matthew 18:1-5).

Ponder verse 5 for a moment before you read on.

'And whoever welcomes a little child like this in my name welcomes me.'

That's why we work in this sphere. We give Christ's love away to others and worship him through our work with children.

The response of the church

The picture we have just seen of God's heart for children is wide-ranging. What can the local church do in concrete terms to respond to the heart cry of a generation that does not know Jesus? Here is a reminder of the seven foundations of our approach. Is my church willing to:

- Make children a priority?
- Equip Christian parents with a range of parenting skills?
- Dedicate resources to activities that build a bridge out to unchurched children?
- Grasp opportunities to participate in the education of children?
- Provoke other churches to similar action?
- Promote culture that uplifts our children?
- Teach our children about compassion, care and justice for children everywhere?

This book explores these seven themes. Let's focus for a moment on 'making children a priority'. This has two expressions. Are children a priority in our overall mission strategy to our neighbourhood? And, are we willing to make the budget commitments that will enable us to implement our strategies and plans?

We deal with the 'priority in mission' question in chapter 3. Part of the reality of our commitment to our children and the children of our communities is however reflected in our budget.

A Children's Ministry survey conducted in 1999 suggested that up to 60% of churches were spending less than £500 on children's work each year. There is significant anecdotal evidence to suggest that the average church is spending about £10 per child per annum. With the average non-Catholic church attendance being 90 and about one third of that being children, the figure of £300 per church seems likely and would bear out the survey findings.

If the church is to make an impact on a new generation of children there will need to be a radical new approach to financing our work with children.

I believe it would be a realistic goal for the church in the

UK to see its number of dedicated children's workers rise from an estimated 500 to 2,000 in the next 10 years. Sunday activities, midweek clubs and schools outreach tasks are sufficient to fill out the workload of a local church worker, even before we begin to explore meeting the social needs of children in our locality and being an advocate for them in the wider political and social arenas.

I believe that if we produce coherent strategies for local children's work that the leadership teams of our churches and the people themselves understand they will give generously.

It will be a sign of the health of the UK church if expenditure in this area becomes a significant and remarked upon item in the coming years.

Money, however, is not the only priority. We will need to work hard to help our churches to see themselves as spiritual nurture centres for children. How might that be demonstrated?

The reality of priorities
Children as a priority will need to be lived out, not simply theorised about.

Here are some provocative questions that a church might want to ask of itself:

• Do the adults in our church greet the children by name?
• Is there any cross-generational conversation?
• In the case of toddlers and younger children, are we willing to crouch down to their level to talk with them?
• Are the facilities we provide for their classes warm, comfortable, age-appropriate and well kept?
• How many times a year does the church leadership meet with the children's ministry team?

27

• Is there a role for a children's activity in the main congregational worship time?

• Do we use younger people and children in servant roles in church life, such as ushering, worship groups and a myriad of other tasks, thus significantly increasing their sense of belonging?

• Do we publicly affirm those who teach the children, in the same way that we honour others in the congregation who undertake major projects or foreign trips?

• Do the children in our church ever get asked to read the Bible publicly or pray?

• If our church prays for people who respond to what God may have said to the congregation, are their children amongst those doing the praying?

We face a huge challenge as we seek to 'reclaim a generation'. Penny Frank, summarises the growing passion of many in *Every Child a Chance to Choose:*

'I want all of us to own the problem as our responsibility. Maybe our local church has a thriving children's work; perhaps we are thrilled at what God is doing through us with children. But I would still like us each to pause where we are and, for a moment, look further afield. I beg you to consider that the way things are going in your church may not be typical of the British Isles as a whole. I would like each reader to be willing to get involved in some way in bringing children's evangelism across the land into a 'better place before God'. Our society is concerned about human rights. That's good. Let me offer this challenge: how can we express genuine concern for the rights of children if we ignore their basic right to their Christian inheritance?

'We need to give them a chance to choose. In calling for every child to have the chance to choose Jesus, I am not campaigning for

28

high-pressure missions or indoctrination programmes. I simply want children to hear the Christian good news in the way that most helps them to understand and absorb it. I don't want them put in a position of dilemma and anxiety. But I do want them to go through their lives knowing how to have an everlasting relationship with God that will enable them to achieve their full potential as human beings'.

Resource list

For further reading
• *Every Child a Chance to Choose* – Penny Frank (Children's Ministry, Kingsway/CPAS). This book is both practical and strategic. Penny is committed to equipping the church to reach the nation.
• *Reclaiming a Generation* – Ishmael (Children's Ministry, Kingsway). Decades of experience distilled into book form. You'll be provoked.

• *The Child in Christian Thought* - Edited by Marcia J Bunge (Eerdmans). A big book covering all the key figures in church history and their perspective on children. For those seeking to clarify their overall thinking on ministry to children this is a landmark book.

• *Biblical Perspectives on Evangelism* – Walter Brueggmann (Abingdon). Worth buying for Chapter 4 on how we pass on the faith to children.

• *Passing on the Faith* – Merton P Stromen/Richard A Hardel (St Mary's Press). This book explores in some depth the role of the family in faith nurture – it is detailed, thoughtful and practical.

• *Children and the Holy Spirit* – Chris Leach (Children's Ministry, Kingsway). A rare gem – so few people write about this important area. If a book can be radical and very sensible at the same time then this one is both.

• *Children in the Heart of God* – David Gidney (Children's Ministry, Kingsway). This is an important book, which examines the perspective of the Old Testament on children. It touches in some depth on wisdom for the parent with respect to spiritual nurture.

• *Children in the Early Church* – W.A Strange (Paternoster Press). A clear and comprehensive guide to New Testament perspectives on children.

Internet
• **www.heartforchildren.com**
The 'articles' section is particularly helpful, with several practical articles alongside helpful academic material.

• **www.dianedew.com/children.htm**
Comprehensive list of scriptures referring to children.

2. Equipping parents to pass on their faith

Knowing that many will feel helpless in the face of contemporary culture and beliefs, we will offer both biblical insight and practical ideas to help parents tell the story of Jesus, celebrate their relationship with God, introduce children to prayer, and offer wise words in the everyday conversations that help plant the seeds of truth.

Equipping parents to pass on their faith

The key to the emergence of a new generation who love God and love his wisdom is the rediscovery of confidence among God's ordained agents of spiritual nurture – Christian fathers and mothers.

If we are to reach a generation of children with the message of God's love expressed through Jesus we must first equip Christian parents to pass on their faith to their own children. These children will in turn become ambassadors to the wider peer network to which they belong.

While many parents instinctively love their children and seek to give them the affirmation and boundary setting

31

that will prepare them for adult maturity, there is perhaps a loss of confidence about their ability to pass on their spiritual values.

Is there an unspoken assumption that Sunday school and midweek clubs will teach our children the stories of faith, and that the atmosphere of church and our often desperate pleas to God for their spiritual protection will help keep them on the straight and narrow?

If we can help our Christian parents discover a more intentional approach to passing on their faith, we can see the emergence of a generation of children who will reach their own friends and peers and be the agents of reformation, revival and renewal in their schools and colleges.

Vital as the role of the trusted adult is in giving truth credibility in the school or youth club context, the trusted child who lets his life shine before his friends is going to have multiple opportunities to let the Spirit speak through him or her.

Our first task is to raise the level of faith amongst parents as to what God can do through children. Let us be quite clear that the child is just as capable of being a prophet, teacher, evangelist, pastor or apostle (Ephesians 4:11) as an adult. The biblical precedents are compelling.

Consider the following. As you do, bear in mind that these are not sideshows along the road of salvation history, but part of the parade of God's power and love that leads us to the life of Christ and his death for our sins.

Samuel

Believed to be between the age of seven and twelve, the young servant to the High Priest is confused as he hears a voice calling to him. Eli, his master and mentor tells him

32

to respond to the voice of God with a willingness to listen.

Samuel receives a message that reveals the corruption at the heart of the nation, and particularly in the household of Eli.

Josiah
He became the king at the age of eight, but was nurtured in the wisdom of God. At the age of sixteen he began to act to clear the pagan worship places from the land.

Naaman's Maid
At his wit's end over his leprosy, the military leader takes the advice of his young maid and goes to see the prophet Elisha.

David
While the nation trembled in fear of the Philistine giant Goliath, David refused the armour of Saul and delivered the Israelites from oppression. The teenage boy went on to become a key figure in salvation history.

Jeremiah
Ordained as a prophet by God, Jeremiah is warned not to use the fact that he is only a child as an excuse. He is given insight and direction for the nation and multiple prophetic words from God.

Joseph
His ability to interpret dreams is a trademark of his life story, but is to have long term impact on the tribes of Israel. He receives the ability while still a youth, but goes on to have significant responsibility in the foreign court in which he finds himself.

Daniel
Daniel and his youthful friends refuse to compromise their beliefs and remain steadfast in their faith. His friends survive a fiery furnace. Daniel is the object of jealously from the king's courtiers but survives their political manoeuvring and is protected by God.

Jesus
Mary and Joseph have to retrace their steps to find the twelve year old Jesus discussing faith with priests and church leaders.

Mary
Mary is widely believed to have been a teenager when she gave birth to Jesus.

The Bible record is very clear. God used children and youth as key figures in salvation history. Are we ready to believe that he can do the same through our children?

What can we do as parents to raise faith-filled, faithful children? There is much that could be written about the nature of parenting. There is clearly a place for emotional support, social boundary setting and the passing on of spiritual values. It's a huge subject.

Are there key insights that will help us begin to under-stand how parents can nurture godly children that might be instruments of God in the same way as the biblical pace setters mentioned above? What can the church do to help resource parents? Here a few habits that might benefit both parent and church.

Seven habits of the effective Christian parent
How you can your church help to nurture parents so that

they in turn nurture their children? They want your encouragement because the Christian parent is often torn between two emotions: love and affection for their child and mild terror. The terror arises from the fear that they are not doing enough/don't know what to do to encourage faith in their children.

Lurking at the back of their mind is an idea that if they don't have regular 'spiritual' conversations with their children, they are somehow failing in their duty. A framework that helps them understand how they can nurture faith can help them, particularly the fathers who are often looking for a recognisable 'plan'.

While the local church may work with the children in any number of contexts, if they also direct their energies to helping parents understand how they can inspire the children, they will multiply the fruit of their teaching many times. With much of our energy in recent decades focused on proper discipline of children, it will also be a helpful balance if we help our parents to inspire as well as control.

So what role can a parent play and what can your church do to support them?

Habit 1 – Be a history teacher
Part of the way we understand life is via our history, the facts, figures and stories of time past. The Bible is in essence the salvation story as it unfolded over thousands of years. It points us to the important role of both an oral and written tradition. Your oral tradition might be your own story of commitment to Christ, the development of your local church or the spiritual exploits of your ancestors.

In Psalm 78:4 the Psalmist promises to 'tell the next generation the praiseworthy deeds of the Lord'. This telling is to pass from generation to generation and seeks to ensure the children would 'put their trust in God and would not forget his deeds but would keep his commands'.

While God has given us wisdom to live by, our faith is at its heart a story. If we simply proclaim the wisdom we are merely moralists. Noted Christian educator John H Westerhoff III writing in *Will our Children have Faith* (Morehouse Publishing) reminds us that:

'At the heart of our Christian faith is a story. And at the heart of Christian education must be this same story. When we evaluate our corporate lives as a community of faith, this story must judge us. Our ritual life, the experiences we have in community, and the acts we perform in the world must be informed by this story. Unless the story is known, understood, owned, and lived, we and our children will not have Christian faith.

The struggle to know, understand, interpret, live, and do God's word must be at the centre of our educational mission. For too long the church in its educational ministry has supported a strange and deafening silence. We have tried to live as if the story were unimportant. Only when the Christian story of God's actions in history becomes the focus of our educational ministry will that ministry be Christian.'

It is a key task of the church to help resource the parent to tell that story.

• *Action – Promote books*

Can your church take action to actively promote Christian books that parents can read to their children or give to them. This can cover everything from Bible stories to figures from history and on into fiction. Reading with children is a relaxed informal way to pass on our faith, and will often provide the environment where we can pass on our own stories of faith.

Habit 2 – Be a parable teller

Raised, as many of us were, in a strong teaching tradition, it can be easy for a parent to talk to children about faith in a 'sermon' style, outlining key beliefs, but not actually communicating.

The role of the story is vital, crossing bridges into people's minds and emotions that simple statements of truth might not. As Jesus tells the story of the Prodigal Son he evokes strong emotions. Anger that a son would wish his father dead, amazement that the son would feed an unclean animal such as a pig, astonishment that the father would show such love to a wayward son. Stories evoke mental images and these tell their own story. The parable of the prodigal doesn't use the word forgiveness but it strongly evokes it.

There is of course a time and place to quote texts to our children but the stories of our lives, the lives of Christian pioneers and other positive storytelling will often leave a more indelible mark.

My children tease me because of my fascination with my family roots in Irish Methodism, but I'm sure they're beginning to understand their place in a historical passing of the faith baton from generation to generation. I'm aware, too, that my parents' admiration of Billy Graham and Hudson Taylor spurred me to read the books about them by Christian biographer John Pollock.

• *Action – Become word artists*

Encourage your church members to spend extra time in the gospels during their personal reading. Read regularly from the gospels in church. Let people become so saturated with the pictures, parables and images that are there that using them becomes second nature.

Encourage church members to research their own family heritage of faith. They may find that even if the immediate family has been far from faith, there have been others who have been followers of Jesus.

Be active in promoting Christian video, such as Miracle Maker, Storytellers, McGee and Me.

If church leadership wants people to discover alternatives to negative culture, they need to become champions of a positive response as well as those who warn of the dangers of contemporary culture.

Habit 3 – Be an example
Jesus modelled Kingdom life to his disciples for three years, leaving a deposit in their lives that enabled them to start a church that would touch the world. Paul urges his readers in the Epistles to follow the example of Christ. Our children will also 'catch' a great deal from our attitudes and responses, both positive and negative.

A variety of Christian thinkers urge parents to help their children understand their thinking not merely follow or obey their example. Parents will not want to be too permissive nor simply authoritarian. Their goal is to raise a child who makes decisions based on a set of values that the child 'owns' as their personal beliefs, not just the thoughts of their parents and friends

Otis and Gail Ledbetter, writing in *Family Fragrance* remind us that our children absorb our influence through every part of their being:

'Family is also experienced through the five senses. Children sense the values of their home with incredible accuracy moment

38

by moment. It is how they first pick up on and process the concept of family, and the place to which they belong. Humans, like every other species, learn by seeing life modelled before their eyes and sensing it through the four other windows of communication.

The place God prepared for that kind of modelling to take place is not the church – as important as it is, nor the school, or children's clubs, or any government institution. God intended people to learn about life in their homes. A wilful newborn eventually becomes a selfless parent by watching his own parents live in a loving manner.'

We know we won't be perfect, but we can negate our own negative behaviour by being ready to apologise and clarify when we do handle a situation badly.

• *Action – Be intentional about parenting support*
Does your church have a one-to-one discipleship programme where people can work through their lifestyle issues in a trusting, prayerful context? Is it possible for your church to promote formal opportunities for groups of parents to talk to each other about the nitty-gritty of parenting?

Is your church promoting a philosophy of parenting, which helps parents understand the proper roles of control and discipline, alongside the need to nurture, love, cherish and encourage their children?

Habit 4 – Be a mentor
Most of us mentor our children. We teach them how to change plugs, make cakes, brew tea, and a host of other tasks. Jesus mentored the disciples, sending them out to pray and then advising them about the tough cases (Luke 10).

Even when we give them the task we often remain with

them to aid them if they falter. They are learning by doing. We are passing on our skills.

It's not always easy for us – some of us want to plan everything. Pre-arranged fatherly or motherly chats might be more our method. Marjorie Thompson, writing in *Family the Forming Center* (Upper Room Books) challenges us about our parenting style:

> 'Years ago I was given a book in which the authors contrasted 'architect parents' and 'farmer parents'. As you might imagine, architect parents have a blueprint in mind for their child. They have often decided (sometimes quite unconsciously) what talents they will encourage and what traits they will not tolerate. The child is expected to follow the parents' expectations for achievement, career, and sometimes even marriage.
>
> Farmer parents, on the other hand, know that their children, like different plants, have different requirements for growth. Just as certain plants require more sun or water than others, some children need more structure or encouragement than others. Farmer parents observe their children's personality traits and talents and learn ways of nurturing each accordingly.'

You will need to be like a farmer – matching children to tasks. You will however discover that they are more capable than we often assume.

At a church I visited recently the nine-piece band, which tackled complex songs, had a 5-year-old drummer. He had been taught by his Dad and was excellent. My own boys have undertaken tasks at the Children's Ministry conferences.

• *Action – Lower the age barrier.*
Make it a key value of your church that all ages can do

most jobs. Encourage parents to 'coach' children in areas where they have similar skills. Turn your children into participants, not spectators in both the home and church.

Habit 5 – Parents as spiritual guides

Throughout the Bible, parents involve their children in the celebration of faith. As the Israelites mourned in the presence of Ezra and Nehemiah they had their children with them. As they moved through the highly symbolic Passover Meal, it took place in a family setting. They took their children to see Jesus on that momentous occasion when he fed 5,000+. They had blessings and prayers for every aspect of life, much of it domestic.

The rituals and traditions can be very straightforward. Author Rolf Garborg wrote *The Family Blessing* (Harrison House) to describe the power of prayer in the home. He writes:

'In our family, the approach we used in blessing our children was quite simple. Each evening at bedtime, I would lay my hands on the head of each of my children and speak the blessing that appears in Numbers 6:24-26, adding at the end the words 'in the name of the Father, and of the Son, and of the Holy Spirit', and personalising it to each child by including his or her name.

It was that simple. We just spoke the same blessing to our children each night. And they came to depend on it as a token of security and a sign of their parents' continuing love for them.

Carlton and Lisa are now adults with children of their own, and amazingly enough, both of them still check in nearly every day to receive their blessing. My children's desire to continue receiving our daily blessing is just one indication of the impact it has made on their lives and on the lives of their children as they pass the blessing on. I know that the family blessing is much more than a bedtime ritual.'

It's simple but profound. The parent can help their child discover the Bible, pray with them, take them to church and visit memorable places where God is at work. They help the child discover the breadth of how God reveals himself to us in Scripture, prayer, the wonders of creation, and the promptings of the Holy Spirit.

• *Action – Promote home based worship*
Model and promote small group prayer and scripture reading. Give people creative and easy to use ideas that they can do at home. Recommend books that will suggest home worship ideas – see resource list at end of chapter.

Habit 6 – Parents as traditionalists
We are surrounded by tradition, particularly festivals such as Christmas or Easter. Your family may have traditional celebrations, such as regular extended family reunions. Our traditions help provide a sense of continuity, structure and security, all of which aid the emotional and intellectual growth of children.

Otis Ledbetter and Tim Smith offer helpful insight in *Family Traditions* (Cook Communications):

'A traditional Jewish prayer asks God for binah, or understanding. The terms is related to bayn, meaning between. This idea is developed in Leo Trepp's book, *The Complete Book of Jewish Observance.*

We have to understand that Judaism has always placed the individual 'between'. We stand between the poles of past and future, between our individual lives and the life of our people in Israel and the world. We are impelled by the love of our forefathers to fashion the future lives of our children. We are called upon to immerse ourselves in society, and, at the same time, to retain our

42

identity as Jews... Each Jew must look at himself or herself and ask, "where do I stand?"

This is a healthy perspective. Instead of being consumed with the individual, there is awareness that I am between. I am between the past and the future. I am between my personal life and the life of my family. I am between my individual life and the life of my faith community. I am between respect for my ancestors and love for my descendants. This awareness is what we call a sense of 'generational place'. When we become aware that our behaviour and values have an impact on generations that follow, we begin to sense a responsibility to pass on a strong heritage. To pass on a heritage to our children, we must first ask, "Where do I stand?"'

• *Action – Your response here can be twofold.*
Reintroduce the Sunday School Anniversary. Celebrate your ministry to children. Model that your church cares about celebrating your history and heritage.

Why not also encourage parents to establish some traditions in the home, weekly special meals or outings where the family can relax together and enjoy each others company? Relaxation and togetherness are a vital prelude to your children's conversations with you about their spiritual questions.

Habit 7 – Seek to be an available parent
In Deuteronomy 6:4 we are urged to speak of God to our children in a wide variety of settings including those times when we are out walking. The key thrust of the text seems to be that wisdom will pass from us to them as we go about the ordinary activities of life, talking and explaining.

I once had a profound discussion with my son about the Devil, while we were sitting waist high in a swimming pool. My other son often talks to me about matters other than our normal diet of football and political gossip when we are walking the dog.

As we help them weigh the pros and cons of the decisions they face or the reality of the dreams that captivate them we are passing on wisdom that will shape their lives for decades. We need to be there however, wasting time with them, idling away afternoons. Our verbal affirmations of love count for something but our presence counts for everything.

An important part of 'being there' relates to the general atmosphere we engender in our homes. Otis and Gail Ledbetter wrote *Family Fragrance* to help describe what this can mean. They use the acrostic **AROMA**.

• **Affection** – A parent's consistent loving out of the will, openly and perhaps spontaneously displayed.

• **Respect** – Holding each family member in honour so that they recognise their true worth.

• **Order** – The art of managing and modelling godly leadership in the home, and the resultant calm that flows from this. This often relates to reliable rhythms of family life.

• **Merriment** – Life was created by God with the intention that it be enjoyed, not endured.

• **Affirmation** – Positive reinforcement of our children whether they've done well or struggled. Encouragement and praise for no reason at all.

• *Action – Have a celebrating parenthood day at church.*
Have a special seminar on the seven habits of the effective parent. Encourage parents to be intentional in their parenting, seeking to be relaxed enough not to regiment their children but deliberate enough to ensure a steady, persistent nurturing of faith.

Resource list

For further reading

• *Passing on the Faith* – Merton P Stromen/Richard A Hardel (St Mary's Press). This book presents a 'radical new model' for youth and family ministry and offers both detailed research and practical solutions. It is built on a 10-part discipleship framework.

• *Family – The Forming Center* – Marjorie J Thompson (Upper Room Books). Beautifully written, profoundly biblical and very practical. I couldn't recommend this book more highly.

• *Family Based Youth Ministry* – Mark DeVries (IVP). Thorough book with many helpful insights into how the Church can help the family be a place of spiritual nurture.

• *Family Time* – Mark and Lindsey Melluish (Kingsway). A new course, which helps parents to discover the gifts of love, teaching and discipline they can give their children

• *Your Heritage* – J Otis Ledbetter/Kurt Bruner (Cook Communications). A warm, anecdotal introduction to a well thought out series. You are introduced to your spiritual, emotional and social legacy, and the week in, week out strategies that will help you pass on your faith and values to your children.

• *The Family Compass* – Kurt and Olivia Bruner (Cook Communications). Helps you address key spiritual concepts via practical down-to-earth conversations and activities

• *Family Traditions* – J Otis Ledbetter and Tim Smith (Cook Communications). How can you help shape your child's 'memories bank', and the understanding of faith that will flow from it? This book will help you.

• *Family Fragrance* – Jo Otis and Gail Ledbetter (Cook Communications). Simple but profound guide to creating a home that reflects your Christian faith in every aspect: Affection, Respect, Order, Merriment and Affirmation are the keys.

• *Spiritual Milestones* – Jim and Janet Weidmann, J Otis and Gail Ledbetter (Cook Communications). Looks at key transitions in life such as Baptism, Communion, Adolescence, Graduation and Marriage, and how a family can mark these times.

• *Celebrations of Faith* – Randy and Lisa Wilson (Cook Communications). Creative, symbolic mini-liturgies, activities and special occasions that will convey faith and hope to your children.

• *Opening your Child's Spiritual Windows* – Cheri Fuller (Zondervan). A treasure chest of ideas, creativity and books lists! This is a pithy and profound book. You'll love it.

• *Feast of Faith* – Kevin and Stephanie Parkes (The National Society). Helpful resource for parents wanting to reinforce the liturgical church calendar with home based activities.

• *The Family Cloister* - David Robinson (Crossroad). Wise, uncomplicated advice for family worship and traditions. Uses the Benedictine Rule as a reference point.

Internet
• **www.youthfamilyinstitute.com**
This web site seeks to offer a comprehensive guide to how the home can be a place of spiritual nurture.

3. Reconnection time – taking Christ to an unchurched generation

We believe that we can bless children by providing opportunities for relaxation, challenge and social interaction. Using many different formats and styles, we will seek in our words and our deeds to 'build a bridge' for truth into their lives.

Reaching the Unchurched Child

The statistics make for harrowing reading. The Sunday School Movement in the UK, which touched the lives of 55% of children every Sunday in 1900, had seen that fall to 32% by 1950 and 4% by 2001 (*Religious Trends 2* - Harper Collins).

The surveys don't always tell the same story, but the picture of decline remains he same. A BBC poll found that 83% of its listeners attended Sunday school during the 1930s-1940s, but only 54% of children attended Sunday school in 1955.

The widely quoted figures of 14% in 1989 and 8% in 1999 are attributed to Christian Research and reflect regular attendance, rather than 'every Sunday' attendance.

What are we to make of this decline into religious indifference by generations of parents and their children? How can we respond?

It's worth digging into the figures a little further, as this will yield signs of hope as well as suggesting that Sunday school statistics are not the whole story

It's also worth noting that the hardest hit by statistical decline amongst adults and children are the mainline denominations such as the Church of England, Church of Scotland, Roman Catholics and Methodists. The Church of England has seen its Sunday school attendance fall by more than 90% since 1950.

The pattern begins to alter when other denominations such as the Baptists, Brethren, New Church and Pentecostals are considered. The Baptist denomination has stabilised numerically in recent years, and has only seen its Sunday schools decline by 65% since 1950. The New Churches and Pentecostals have seen sustained growth throughout the last 50 years, and could soon have the second largest Sunday school movement of all denominations – they are currently in third place behind the Anglicans and Baptists. (Source – *Religious Trends 2* - Harper Collins).

If we are going to reach the unchurched child we must first examine the host of factors that have led to decline and enquire as to why some groups have seen growth.

Why the decline?

Theological
In denominational structures strongly influenced by liberal theological thought, there is often a loss of passion for the unchurched or nominal. While some believe that uncertainty

doesn't attract people to church, it's even more likely that it will demotivate those still there.

Generational drift
No exhaustive surveys exist to validate the following claim, but it could be argued that many religious people of parenting age have drifted into the Renewed Anglican, Baptist, New Church and Pentecostal churches. Their relative buoyancy with respect to 'Sunday school' style activities reflects the prevalence of 30-40 year olds amongst their ranks.

It also tends to produce a 'virtuous circle', as there is often the personnel, manpower and passion to reach out to the unchurched child.

Theological pragmatism
I would argue, however, that until the last decade, many Evangelical churches had lost sight of an urgent vision for the unchurched child. This was partly related to a loss of tradition. Many transferred into new structures, while the tradition bearers remained in the old denominations.

There was also a strong 'family service' movement within Anglicanism that mirrored theological thinking throughout the church. Their reasoning was as follows:

• The Bible and therefore the Church values the family.

• Therefore we should stop trying to reach the individual child and seek to reach whole families.

• Children who find faith, but have parents who don't embrace that faith, will find themselves in a hostile environment. Many will not persevere.

49

• Therefore, the logic goes, evangelise adults who will bring in their children.

The flaw in all of this, of course, is that many adults now have no clue about Christian orthodoxy, because they never attended church as a child, and are that much more difficult to reach. Those who do have some link with faith through three-times a year attendance are being reached by the Alpha course project that has been used by 7,000 UK churches. Parenting and marriage courses are now being run by many churches looking for a new 'fringe' to feed their Alpha, or similar, courses.

Alpha is, however, a phenomena of the last seven years. For nearly 25 years or more there was little or no consensus on how to reach the unchurched child.

Cultural factors
The authority of the Church as a bearer of God's Word has been under sustained attack since the 1960s. We won't dwell on this here, but it's important to note the following factors in our overall thinking.

• Science – While many question the authority of science now, it has for many decades disputed the claims of Christ and denigrated the supernatural.

• Sexuality – The culture has given itself permission to explore sexuality outside of committed, for better or for worse, relationships. The Church's stance has been seen as repressive.

The fruit, however is the disintegration of the traditional two parents, 'married for life' family unit. This has had huge implications for the Sunday school movement.

Many children who might have attended for an hour on Sunday are now with the 'other parent' on a weekend access visit.

• Spirituality – The rebirth of a high profile paganism gives people permission to discover spirituality of many different types. People are keen to explore the spiritual but loath to commit to an institution. The growth of astrology, alternative medicine, wiccan paganism, and the vast array of spirituality in the Mind, Body and Spirit section of your local bookstore, further suggests the marginalisation of the Church in the minds of many. The rather less formal commitment demanded by the literature of self-help and self-discovery suits a consumer generation whose focus is themselves, not their community.

• Irrelevance – If the liberal churches held out a doubting faith, the evangelicals often held out an intransigent one. Often authoritarian in nature, they did not explain the wisdom of God's Word, but reminded you that God had said it, so you should do it – quite unlike their mentors, Jesus and Paul, who discussed faith in marketplaces, homes and fishing boats.

The everyday activities that embedded churches in a local community were often despised because they were identified as being an expression of the 'social gospel', or simply not direct enough in calling people to a faith decision. These embedded activities often involved children (Parents and Toddlers, Uniformed Groups).

The churches with something to say and a reason to say it were often in retreat from a hostile and fast-changing world. There was a deeply pragmatic approach to contact with the unchurched. 'How quickly can you ask them about their spiritual state?', seemed to be the key question.

An inarticulate, scared church had little reason to risk itself for the lost children of a generation, and only its most extreme members tried. It's from these extremes, however, that the strategies for today have arisen, and it's to them we will return shortly.

Methods
Could it be that the churches communication methods also left something to be desired? The prevalence of a rhetorical 'preaching' method in many churches may have spilled over into the Sunday school. It will be the work of others to chart the growth of teaching materials that reflected the growing importance of the visual, and how Christian thinking in this area advanced. How many did we lose, however, before we began to update our curriculum and methods?

The situation today is that most churches use a curriculum that seeks to take account of the visual learner, the tactile (let me do a craft or activity) learner and the auditory learner (just tell me the story). It also seeks to meet, via four-step lesson plans, the different types of motivation that a child has. One child wants the facts, another wants to know why she needs the facts, another wants activities that reflect these facts, and yet another wonders what he will do with this information in the coming week.

The tide is turning
If we are to share the good news of Jesus with an unchurched generation we must first question whether the situation is as bleak as the preceding pages might suggest, clarify our mission foundations, and then look at some case studies and role models.

Glimmers of light

When analysing the statistics we must first answer some questions. How much of the decline in recent years relates to delayed child bearing within the general population? Is there a 'gap' simply because many women are bearing children ten years later than has historically been the case? This also begs the question as to whether some of the decline in Sunday attendance also relates to smaller family sizes.

I'm not aware of a significant survey that seeks to introduce these factors into a discussion.

Midweek Culture

The Church is finding that midweek contact with children is a more viable option. There are a variety of reasons:

• Family mobility – The growing culture of weekends away and Sunday as family day – especially where the parent/parents are working hard throughout the week – makes weekday activities more attractive.
• After school and evening activities are seen as 'community service' by many local authorities anxious to help the working parent and provide positive environments for children.
• Many families are positive about a week-night culture of activities for their children and already take them to several diferent things.
• Many churches do not have the volunteers to staff a large Sunday children's ministry. Their existing Sunday volunteers are nevertheless committed enough to take on a midweek club as well.

National church reports and surveys have noted that this is a way forward for the local congregation. It would be good if, in the next five years, we could begin to quantify the reach of these midweek activities, and see what the impact is on the percentage of children reached when we move beyond simply measuring the Sunday morning attendance figures.

This chapter will shortly examine some of the creative ways that local congregations are using to build bridges into children's lives. First things first, however. On what biblical foundations are we building our mission ideas? It seems to me that the following will be key.

Mission foundations

We have to love where we live.
In many cases this will involve concentrating on the streets immediately around our building, rather than the more heroic task of 'reaching the whole town' for Jesus.

We will often have a physical presence in those streets. This relates to both our buildings and our people. Friendship grows and deepens as the children who may attend your church clubs meet you in the everyday course of life.

It will help if we can recapture the Biblical sense of place. The Bible mentions 'land' over 1,700 times. Chronicles tells us that part of the fruit of humility and repentance will be that God will heal our land (2 Chronicles 7:14).

Here are some principles to ponder as you think about the place where you live:

• God wants you to be at home in his creation and the place he leads you to. Read Psalm 23. Where are the pleasant places where you live?

• God wants to give you a reputation there (Luke 4:23-28; John 1:46). Contrast the reputation of Nazareth and the promise of God in Psalm 112. Does your church have a reputation with local children and parents?

• God uses social networks as carriers of the good news. Jesus' fame spread through Galilee (Mark 1:28). Simon the sorcerer, despite his fame, was drawn to faith by the reputation of Philip as a man of God (Acts 8:12-13). Your children will draw in dozens of others via their social networks.

• Ordinary people can be at the centre of a community. Your active compassion will speak volumes, at work or in the community (Acts 9:35-43; 16:14). The church is still by far the largest provider of voluntary youth and children's activities in most communities in the UK. Organisations such as Faithworks are seeking to quantify this, but their founder Steve Chalke told a London media briefing that, in the youth sector alone, UK churches employed over 7,000 compared to 3,000 employed by local government.

Love the people where we live
This may seem blindingly obvious, but it's not always the case. If we've steeped ourselves in a theology which only reminds us of our alienation from the world, the perversion of goodness by sin, the coming judgements of God and the strong possibility of endless torment in the fires of hell, then we may come across to most people as the tiniest bit judgemental.

Sin, separation and judgement are important to our overall understanding of God's unfolding relationship with us, but they won't usually be at the forefront of our minds in our everyday interaction with non-Christians.

Jesus was trusted by the ordinary people of his day because his first contacts with them were often filled with grace and acceptance. He invited himself to the tax-collectors house, and allowed his feet to be washed by a woman. He touched the diseased and embraced every class in his society with friendship. As many as fifteen of the gospel incidents or parables refer to eating, a sure sign of acceptance and social bridge building.

Some of this 'mixing with publicans and sinners' was not well received by the religious of the day, who regarded many of Jesus' friends as ritually impure. Jesus' love attracted the anger of many, but also drew to him many alienated by the conventional religion of the day.

The pattern we observe in Luke 10 may be profoundly helpful as we seek to understand how to reach children and their families.

He instructs the 72, as they go out, to:

• **Declare peace** – they were to pray for God's peace to come to that place. Their praying for the goodness of God to be made manifest was a positive form of spiritual warfare, declaring to the forces of darkness that a new spiritual day had dawned. As we pray for the children of our district we are declaring peace over them. We can pray for them when we see them on the street, when they enter our clubs and when we stop to pray for the projects we are involved in. They may never hear our prayers but God will.

• **Eat with people** – relationship is built through relaxed conversation and the giving and receiving of hospitality. One youth worker told me that a school club she was taking changed completely when they abandoned the normal format and simply ate together. Everyone was more relaxed and conversation flowed.

• **Pray for their needs** – people are often open to prayer in a way that they are not open to more conventional faith sharing.

• **Declare that the kingdom of God is near** – finally comes the sharing about a new relationship with God and a new way of living.

We have historically reversed the order. Can I share my faith with you? Let me pray for you. By the way, why not come for a meal; may the Lord bless you.

The Luke 10 order allows trust to grow. The only way we will reach this generation is by regaining their friendship and trust. They don't want to be evangelism targets; they want to be friends. If they trust us and trust our church, they'll visit and they will let their children visit. As long as they don't feel coerced, they'll see and hear the Word from our lives and our words.

This love for the people where you live is the bedrock of the work of the Frontline church in Liverpool. They run Kidz Klubs several times a week in and around the city. They don't tour the country urging others to do likewise. If you want to find out more you have to go and visit them.

The Message to Schools trust in Manchester have a similar ethos. Despite worldwide fame for their Message Tribe dance music band, they don't take bookings outside of Manchester during term time. Loving the people where you are is a cardinal value for them.

Tell me the story
Another vital strand in our thinking relates to the power of story. Jesus expressed much of his teaching in stories or

memorable poems, such as the Sermon on the Mount. Even today, the idea of the Good Samaritan or the Prodigal Son still figure in popular speech.

A story released into a child's mind will often stay with them for the rest of their lives. This will be particularly important for the unchurched child. We can admonish them about living good lives and obeying the golden rule, but they are more likely to remember and retain a story and its view of reality.

A local church in my home town sponsored the showing of *Miracle Maker* for pupils of a local school. This animated pilgrimage through the life of Christ held their attention and drew them into the life of the Saviour. So strongly did some identify with the hero – Jesus – that they shouted out when it became clear he was going to be crucified. They were appalled at the injustice of it all – why should a good man die?

A group of churches in Bedford combined their resources to sponsor and staff the reading of Bible stories to children in local school assemblies. This was born of their desire to give the children a vocabulary of faith – a basic understanding of the Christian story – out of which all other conversations can flow.

Points of Contact
Whatever our methods and our theology, a willingness to use many different 'points of contact' will be vital.

What is the size of the task?
In our church, most of the congregation live in two distinct electoral wards around the building where we meet. We have a heart for the whole town, but we're concentrating our energy on these two wards.

Using the 2001 census, we are going to discover how many children and youth there are in our area. It's likely to be about 3,000 out of the 15,000 population. We're then going to spend time with all the other churches in the area and clarify how many attend our Sunday and midweek activities, including some of our community projects.

We will then examine the impact of our schools work. A picture will emerge about how many are being reached at the moment, which will enable us to establish a base line or starting point. We can then clarify how we might reach others and set goals for the next 15 years.

The overarching goal is intentional contact in a variety of contexts with all the children in our area, via the local network of churches.

Your church can make a difference. Here are some ideas, case studies and thought-starters for you. They combine a multitude of approaches, rather than a single strategy.

Families reaching families
The 'reach a family, reach a child' argument may have slowed our outreach, but it doesn't mean it is without merit. Many reading this book will know that 'school gate' and 'school friends' networks are key strands in the local community web. A long term commitment to hospitality, prayer and friendship will open the door to faith for some of your spiritually curious friends and their children.

The church or cell group can support this with community events, such as picnics, fun days, barbecues and other gatherings, where your community friends get to meet your church friends. Attending your church at some point in the future will not seem so strange if they already know half a dozen families.

Peer group positive
Peer group influence brought Nathaniel into the discipleship group surrounding Jesus. Matthew introduced Jesus
to his fellow tax collectors. This should remind us that the
most potent evangelists amongst young people and children
are our own children. You can't plan strategies for them to
reach their friends, but you can pray daily for them and
with them.

When they tell us about issues their friends are facing,
or questions they are asking, we can help provide answers
or stop and pray for the specific needs of that person. This
models compassion and concern and will often lead your
child to pray for the needs, unprompted by you.

Not every child in your church or family will have a
'gathering in' personality, but the ones who do will bring
many to your church based activities. Even the quiet ones
may still bring one or two of their friends.

It can be tempting to want to pull our children away from
the negative atmospheres surrounding some of their
school friends. We may need to believe, however, that our
positive character building in their lives, our emotional
support and our prayers will actually enable them to be
like pastors, prophets, evangelists, teachers and apostles
in the situations they enter.

Is it not possible that we might taint the world with
goodness, because 'He that is in us is greater than he that
is in the world' (1 John 4:4)?

Conventional activities
There will always be some interest in the conventional
Sunday School/Junior Church, and the Bible orientated
midweek activity. There are still parents who are willing

to let their children come to these activities, and your own children's network will always draw some in. Consider these types of activity as another arrow in your quiver.

Bridge activities
The home is not the only arena where new friendships are started or strengthened. In Bible times the marketplace was often the venue where discussion took place, strangers introduced themselves to the wider community and hospitality was offered.

The church has many unique opportunities to express its heart for the locality by unconditional acts of service expressed in the local places where people gather. They are unconditional because they are offered as a blessing to the locality, not simply as a means of 'evangelising' people. But the reality is that for many they will be a 'marketplace' or 'threshold' where they encounter Christians and begin to discover new friendships.

Laurence Singlehurst, writing in *Sowing, Reaping, Keeping* reminds us that the 40 who attend a parent and toddler club may produce ten who attend a parenting course, from whom five attend an Alpha course, or some other similar introduction to faith project. We still want to bless the 35 whatever their response to faith, but the five needed a neutral situation where they could observe faith in action and start their pilgrimage.

So what do these bridge activities for children look like? Here is a snapshot of the types of activities one local church supports. There are about 80 adults in the church.

• **Live Wires** – up to 40 children attend an activities/sports based youth club, which concludes with a short epilogue.
• **Kids Plus** – this Saturday afternoon family club has an

61

attraction for several different types of family. Some attend because of the availability of table tennis and pool. For others, particularly divorced parents on access visits to their children, it's a great place to spend an hour or two together while having the use of a wide variety of toys, games and sports equipment.

• **Wise Up** – this weeknight club is aimed at girls and offers them a chance to relax together, enjoy the facilities of the centre and spend some time looking at issues that face a teenage girl, such as self-image, sexuality and self-respect. It's a sexual abstinence orientated programme.

• **Parents & Toddlers** – many, many churches have them. It blesses the local young mothers and reminds the local community that you are still alive and viable as a church. It familiarises people with your building.

Proclamation activities
Many churches around Europe are finding that a full-blown major production allied to a direct sharing of Christian truth will still attract hundreds of unchurched children on a regular basis.

The Kidz Klub model has been pioneered in the UK by the Frontline church in Liverpool. Working with other churches in the immediate locality, they now reach over 2,000 children a week. The majority of the Kidz Klubs take place on weekday late afternoons, early evenings, or Saturday mornings

Kidz Klub worker Celia Morris summarises their programme. 'It breaks down into three sections. We start with high energy praise and then have a games/action time, before moving into the core "message" time.'

They use a variety of media and a fast paced approach. The teaching is very focused. 'We have one memory verse and one key point each week. We want the children to grasp something that they can live out.'

Frontline, the host church, is not a 'mega-church', but has recruited dozens of volunteers to help the small group of full time staff.

The heartbeat of the Kidz Klub model is a trust-building exercise with the local people. The team visit the household of every child once a week. The doorstep encounters may be as brief as twenty seconds, but they may last several minutes as sick family members are prayed for and day-to-day life issues are discussed.

They often lead to more contact with the wider family and help place the church in the minds of local people as the 'lead institution'. This in turn makes the church a place to seek support and spiritual guidance for the whole family.

Kidz Klub worker Dave Sharples told Children's Ministry magazine, 'We don't pretend to know all the answers, but what we do know is that what God is doing in our city will result in real regeneration. Money, houses and facilities are very important, but it is only when people are changed on the inside that they discover true hope for the future.

Signs of hope
In a survey, which attracted responses from over 1,000 churches, Children's Ministry discovered that as the millennium turned, as many as 44% of churches were seeing growth in their Sunday work with children. 23% were stable. Churches reported growth in all the key midweek activities, such as Toddler groups, Clubs, Uniformed organisations, Children's cells, and Playgroups. Particularly noticeable was the growth in churches establishing new projects.

Children's work advocate Penny Frank encourages people to look at what the community needs, not just what the church might like to do. 'The idea of the serving church really needs to come back into force again. How can we help families in our community?'

Which brings us full circle to Robert Raikes. Widely regarded as the father of the Sunday school movement, his original motivation related to a desire to help quell the listless hooliganism of many children on a Sunday. He wanted to bring education to working class children, using the Bible and the church catechism. He met the need of the local community, using a 'bridge' activity. This had a secondary benefit of reminding children for many generations of their spiritual foundations.

And finally
Our intention in reaching out to the unchurched child could be summarised as follows:

• To serve the local community by blessing children and parents with a variety of resources and events.

• To let that same group of people know that we love them unconditionally.

• To share the story of Jesus, thereby providing a vocabulary of faith, which can play a part in all our ongoing dialogue with someone throughout the rest of their lives.

• To introduce young people to the wisdom of God, expressed through the Bible and explain why it makes sense.

• To remind a generation of the concept of right and wrong, and help them think of their decisions in terms of values, not expediency.

• To call a generation to follow Jesus wholeheartedly, turning away from their rebellion, seeking God's forgiveness and joining with others as they seek to serve him.

The tide is turning

Resource list

For further reading
• *Every Child A Chance To Choose* – Penny Frank (Children's Ministry/Kingsway/CPAS). Moves from the visionary to the practical and includes dozens of case studies.

• *Whose Child Is This?* – Bill Wilson (Charisma House). The poignant, but inspiring story of the founder of the Kidz Klub movement and the 23,000 strong Kidz Klub in New York.

• *100 Ideas For Midweek Clubs* – Jan Dyer (Kingsway). Games, activities and much more for your midweek activities.

• *ALF – About Life & Faith* (Viz-a-Viz) A resource pack to help churches take the massage of Jesus to unchurched children.

• *MiniZone, KidZone, Y-Zone* (Children's Ministry Teaching Programme) A curriculum to help you disciple the children in your church.

Internet
• **www.chancetochoose.com**
This site is updated regularly with fresh features and insights into how to reach the children of this generation.

Contacts
• **Kidz Klub**, PO Box 38, Wavertree, Liverpool L15 0FH; Tel: (0151) 733 3373

From Foundations To Strategies

So far, we've sketched out an underlying ethos for ministry to children, the role of the parent and a foundation for mission to the unchurched.

What follows are four key thought-starter chapters. These will give you direction and perhaps provoke you as you explore the following key questions:

• How can we reach our schools?

• How can we create an ongoing awareness of the importance of children's ministry?

• How can we help our children discover positive and uplifting culture?

• How can we be advocates for the child in our wider culture and society?

4. Being salt and light in our schools

Just as Jesus and his contemporaries learnt practical knowledge and eternal truth at the synagogue school in Nazareth, we understand that we have an opportunity to tell the Christian story and speak of Christian values through the school system. Through our own resources, and in coalition with other like-minded churches, we commit to helping every child, in every school in our locality, to hear the Good News of Jesus several times during their formal education.

Taking God to school
The church has historically been a leader in the pioneering of education. The ancient monasteries were centres of learning and education and produced both priests and politicians, craftsmen and geographers, soldiers and artists.

Inspired by education pioneer and church leader Comenius, church groupings took education beyond the monastery. Through European universities, such as Halle, they began to offer education to both the ordinary working people and to girls.

The advent of the Sunday school movement, pioneered by Robert Raikes in the late 18th Century produced a significant new era in British society, as many ordinary children were given the opportunity to learn how to write and write for the first time. Social reformer Lord Shaftesbury opened 'Ragged Schools' in London to offer more formal education during the week.

The Church continued to be a pioneer of education, with the Church of England establishing schools throughout the country. By the time the 1944 Education Act bought schools under the influence of central government almost a third of the schools in the UK had been established by the Church. This remains the situation today.

This heritage is thought by many to have been lost. Debates about the content of contemporary state sponsored education are commonplace. Education is not deemed to be a neutral sphere and political, social and humanistic agendas such as environmental action and contraceptive advice are often advanced via the curriculum.

Christian schools have, however, often fared well in the academic achievement tables. The praise heaped on Emmanuel College in Gateshead by leading Labour politicians did not preserve it from a media onslaught when it became clear that the school regarded evolution as just a theory and preferred to teach a creationist worldview.

So how are Christians to interact with the educational sphere? Many Christians are increasingly comfortable with the idea of 'confessional pluralism' (CP). This can be summarised as follows:

• Different voices with different worldviews have the right to be heard in every sphere of society.

• This is not because they are all equally valid or right, but because freedom of speech and expression is a high value for Christians and should be defended for all.
• This is emphatically not a multi-faith, all roads lead to God approach. This is a 'St Paul was happy to debate his beliefs on Mars Hill (Acts 17)' approach.

CP helps Christians of every hue feel comfortable within public institutions. Not all feel at ease with the idea of a state religion and its imposition upon schools via legislation. CP reminds us however that we should have a seat at the educational table.

It is important for Christians to be involved with their local schools for several reasons:

• It gives us the chance to tell children the story of Jesus.
• It allows us the opportunity to speak into debates about morality. These issues are at the heart of Religious Education and Personal Social Education lessons.
• It gives our children the opportunity to be positive influences on their peers. (It would be interesting to do a survey on how many head boy/girls come from Christian homes.)
• Schools are at the centre of many informal networks. The playground is a 'threshold' or 'marketplace' where new friendships form for both child and adult.
• It allows us to participate in national and local debates about education.

As churches consider their participation in the local community and their commitment to reaching children, there will be myriad opportunities to touch lives in the education environment.

Emlyn Williams, head of Scripture Union in Schools, has words of wisdom for those seeking to influence their local schools. Writing in the CPAS Leadership magazine he comments:

'Partnership: How do things look from the school's point of view? In many schools there is a real openness to help from the community. They recognise that education is a partnership and look for all the help that they can get. Not only that, they are legally charged with responsibility for the spiritual, social moral and cultural development of pupils. Those are areas where church have most expertise and resources to share.

'At the same time, schools can be suspicious of our agenda. When we work in schools we are on someone else's territory. (The headteacher and governors have final responsibility) and have to be able to handle that context, so we need to be open and honest and listen to how they express their needs. Working in partnership with other churches wherever possible can be more acceptable to schools, as well as challenging the common idea that churches can't work together.'

There is growing commitment to establishing more church based schools. An official report entitled *Way Ahead – Church of England Schools in the New Millennium* has challenged the Anglican Church to establish 100 new secondary schools in the next seven years. The report also calls for an unspecified number of new primary schools and notes:

'Expansion of provision is not enough. To be at the heart of the Church's mission, church schools must be distinctively Christian. Nor can church schools be fully engaged in the Church's mission at parish level, unless they are in close partnership with the worshipping community.'

The report also calls for better training for ministers with respect to schools work, and a major effort to encourage Christians to become teachers in these schools as a vocational choice.

What can I do?
Here are some things your church might like to do, start or support.

Schools value voluntary assistance in the following areas:

• Collective worship (assemblies)
• Reading support and classroom assistance
• Adults to assist with camps and trips
• Adults with specific expertise who can participate in Religious Education and Personal Social Education lessons.

Schools may welcome specialist projects that help them with problem or at risk pupils:

• Specialist help for excluded children.
• Self image/self worth/sexual attitudes teaching.

Schools also appreciate church support in practical ways:

• The CLC bookshop chain run a Books4schools project that enables churches to put a £100 or £200 package of books into schools. Publishers participate and the value of the books is often considerably more.
• Schools are often wanting to recruit governors. Care for Education provides specialist training for people willing to invest their time in this task.

• School Clubs – schools may be willing for your church, or a representative of local Christians, to help facilitate midday or after school clubs. These may have an explicitly Christian ethos and give an opportunity to share the Christian narrative.

Your church could encourage the following:

• Prayer for teachers and all involved in education – many churches set aside a special time once a year for public prayer.

• News of work in schools in your church bulletin.

• Spreading information about specific prayer groups for schools in your locality.

We have an opportunity to be salt and light in our schools. Let's take it.

Resource list

For further reading
• *Effective Schools Work* – Lee Jackson
(Kingsway Communications)

• *The Schools Work Handbook* – Emlyn Williams
(Scripture Union)

• *Running Christian Groups in Schools* – Esther Bailey
(Scripture Union)

• *School Assemblies Need You!* – Richard Dyter (Monarch)

Further help is available from

• **Scripture Union in Schools**, 207-209 Queensway, Beltchley, Milton Keynes MK2 2EB. Tel: (O1908) 856000

• **Association of Christian Teachers**, 94a London Road, St Albans AL1 1NX. Tel: (01727) 840298.

• **CARE for Education**, 53 Romney Street, London SW1P 3RF. Tel: (0171) 233 0455.

• **Stapleford House Education Centre**, Wesley Place, Stapleford, Nottingham NG9 8PD. Tel (0115) 939 6270.

Internet
• Books4Schools
www.clc.org.uk/books_for_schools.cfm

• Care for Education
www.care.org.uk/dept/education

• ACT
www.christian-teachers.org

• The Stapleford Centre
www.stapleford-centre.org

5. Working together to reach a generation

If the people of God are to grasp the nettle and make a difference to this generation of children, we will need to ensure that child-friendly mission thinking permeates the Church.

Those responsible for leadership are key. Penny Frank, of the Church Pastoral Aid Society (CPAS) has spent the last two years visiting Bishops in the Church of England and urging them to ensure that children are a priority in their planning. She will eventually see every Bishop and many church leaders from other denominations.

She is emphatic in her call:

Of course, not every church leader must be skilled and competent in working with children. But unless all leaders are concerned for this area in the life of their church, unless they are actively encouraging its success and well being, they are not effectively leading that church. The disciples their church makes will be adults; the children growing up around that church will never have the chance to choose Jesus.

Church leaders and lay people need to be equipped for the

task with practical, inspirational and theological training. What foundations will we be building on with respect to training?

Practical and Inspirational

The last five years have seen a significant increase in training and teaching for the children's ministry volunteer. In addition to the long term popularity of Scripture Union training activities, we have seen the growth of the annual Children's Ministry conference, which attracts between 1500-2,000 annually to Eastbourne. Children's Ministry also sponsor regional training days. Almost every speaker at the conference also participates in local church or diocesan related training throughout the year.

The short punchy and practical seminars on offer in these contexts often release new thinking and creativity at a local level, and have led to increased use of puppets, fresh ideas for children and prayer, and many other small innovations.

This type of training, aimed at the busy lay person, would seem to be in robust health. We should not, however, be lulled into a false sense of security. What is the health of the theological wells that supply the practical streams?

Thinking theologically

There is much to encourage us in this sphere too, as you will discover when you read on. But the task is significant. Penny Frank, writing in *Every Child a Chance to Choose* warns:

> As far as the normal courses for theological training of our main denominations are concerned, not one of the colleges I have approached has been able to claim that their theological study

will include the young. For example, a course may include a module on pastoral care, but it is unusual to find a component on the pastoral care of children within it. Study of the subject of bereavement might include the issue of caring for adults bereft of a child. It does not usually include the issue of caring for a bereaved child. Even where a course director ensures that the subject of children is introduced at some time during a course, it is likely that the chosen topic will be the nurture of children in the church. The chosen topics are more likely to be Sunday groups, children and communion, or all-age worship.

The challenges for us are very clear:

• Will those who study theology include reflection on all ages in their application of that truth?

• Will all concerned with Christian publishing and academia work to ensure a growing body of literature on a theology of childhood? The resource lists in this book mention some of the titles beginning to emerge, but there needs to be many more if further study in this vital area is to flourish.

It's worth noting, however, that there has been a slow but steady growth of new child related courses in UK Bible colleges.

Moorlands Bible College, Cliff College and St John's Extension Studies have helped lead the way with specific Children's Work courses that combine, in varying amounts, residential study and distance learning.

Here is a snapshot of the areas being explored:

• **Cliff College** – *Diploma Course in Children's Evangelism and Nurture.* This is a joint project with Scripture Union.

Subjects covered include The Place of Children in God's Kingdom, The Child and Spirituality, Communicating with Children.

• **Oak Hill College** – *Youth and Children's Ministry Course.* This course has a particular emphasis on pastoral care and the integration of children into the wider life of the church.

• **Leading Children** – *Distance Learning.* Academically grounded by its roots at St John's College, Nottingham, this course is being promoted by Kingsway's Children's Ministry as an ideal tool for those wanting to stretch their thinking, but unable to undertake full-time training.

• **University College Chichester** – *Degree Courses.* The University is looking to launch courses in the Theology and Practice of Youth and Children's Ministry at certificate, diploma, degree and post-graduate level.

What can I do?
All of the activity mentioned above is like green shoots in a barren valley. But we need to plant and water for several decades if we are to see the full flowering of God's plan for children.

With five or six church institutions now alert to the issues surrounding ministry to children, the initiative now lies with the ordinary lay person such as you and I. Will we be champions of ministry to children within our sphere of influence? Will we be willing to work within our denomination, diocese or town to promote positive models of children's ministry? Will we work with all involved in training in our church grouping to bring this vital area higher up on the agenda?

Here are some questions to help you think through how you might take action:

• Does my church grouping or denomination have a children's officer, co-ordinator or trainer? If so, when can I meet him/her?

• Is my church grouping sponsoring or recommending any training? Could I help initiate it?

• Does my grouping have an explicit statement of intent with respect to ministry to children?

• Is children's ministry discussed or resourced at the annual gatherings of my church grouping?

• Does my denomination or grouping have a budget for resourcing ministry to children?

• What help do the training colleges associated with my church circle offer both to minister and dedicated children's ministry workers? Who would be the best person to dialogue with about this?

The singer Sam Cooke sang 'A change is going to come'. I believe that it is in this key area. You are part of that change.

Resource List

For further reading:
• **Churches' Child Protection Advisory Service** (CCPAS)
PO Box 133, Swanley, Kent BR8 7UQ. Tel: 0845 1204550
www.ccpas.org.uk

• **Cell Church**
For information about cell church, contact Cell Church UK.
www.cellchurch.co.uk

Colleges and training
• **Children's Ministry,** Lottbridge Drove, Eastbourne BN23 6NT. Tel: 01323 437748
www.childrensministry.co.uk

- **Cliff College**, Calver, Hope Valley, Sheffield S32 3XG
Tel: 01246 582321
www.cliffcollege.org

- **London Bible College**, Green Lane, Northwood HA6 2UW.
Tel: 01923 456000
www.londonbiblecollege.ac.uk

- **Oak Hill College**, Chase Side, Southgate, London N14 4PS.
Tel: 0208 449 0467
www.oakhill.ac.uk

- **Scripture Union**, 207-209 Queensway, Bletchley, Milton
Keynes MK2 2EB. Tel: 01908 856111
www.scriptureunion.org.uk

- **Moorlands College,** Sopley, Christchurch BH23 7AT. Tel:
01423 672 369
www.moorlands.ac.uk/specialist.htm

- **University College Chichester,** College Lane, Chichester,
PO19 6PE. Tel: 01243 816193
www.ucc.ac.uk
At the time of writing there are no details about the proposed
course on the web site, but information can be found on
www.ishmael.org.uk

6. Releasing a sense of wonder

We will intentionally seek out and promote to our children, (via home and church) music, reading and other cultural expressions of a Biblical faith. We will by this means impart a sense of wonder; a God centred way of seeing and a joy in believing. We do this as a response to the theft of their innocence by some aspects of mass media culture. We will also seek to help our children discern popular culture, recognising and responding to that which seeks for truth, and rejecting that which celebrates evil or deception.

Culture that Uplifts

If there is one area of contemporary life that has been a constant irritant in the church's spiritual wounds, it is popular culture.

Churches routinely disapprove of it. Parents are often in inner turmoil as they wrestle with how to cope with the conflict it can cause in the home.

If we are to help parents we must first establish our stance on culture from a biblical perspective. We must then help our children learn to be discerning about culture. Our final task will be to promote and encourage positive culture.

A biblical view of culture

Discussing this could take many chapters. Let me briefly state a perspective.

God has created us in his image. As he created man and all around him, he constantly reflected that it was good (Genesis 1). He revealed his word through majestic poetry, highly pictorial prophecy and dramatic historical dealings with the people of Israel. The temple he allowed Solomon to build was visually magnificent – as is the vision of heaven which unfolds in the book of Revelation.

Many Christians are however wary of the arts. This is often rooted in the incursion of Greek thought into Christian thinking. This elevates the mind and the spirit and denigrates physical reality. It strongly encourages the idea that some activity is sacred and some secular. This leads many to believe that the church must not use 'the methods of the world' or 'the devil's music'.

This does not do justice to either history or Scripture. History suggests that the pioneers of radio in America were Christian broadcasters. The first widely distributed popular book was Bunyan's *Pilgrim's Progress*. (Huge publishing houses such as HarperCollins, Hodder & Stoughton and Bertlesmann all have their roots in Christian publishing companies of the last century.)

In reality what often happens is that the church expresses and communicates about God and Jesus creatively, giving their creative gifts back to God as an act of worship. The rest of society will, however, use those same art forms for idolatrous purposes. The church is not using the world's methods – the world is abusing God's good gifts.

The 'people of the Book' should not hesitate, therefore, to use books, music, art, dance and a variety of forms to express their worship to God and the view of life that flows from it.

Learning to discern

There will nevertheless be much about popular culture that deeply disturbs. Owners of a Sky satellite dish will know that the selection of music channels available gives a 24-hour platform to the innocent and the idealistic alongside the inane and profane.

Helping a child think carefully about the latest pop video is a way of blessing them. If you help them think by asking them a question, they will begin to 'own' their decisions about what they listen or watch. If you explain the wisdom behind your thinking you begin to help them understand the world, not merely follow your commands. A child who knows 'why' is much more likely to make the same decision when they are away from your influence.

This is not the place for detailed cultural analysis, but the resources list below will help you begin to explore the discernment idea yourself. I would particularly recommend Plugged In – http://www.family.org/pplace/pi for thoughtful overviews of contemporary films and music.

In this sample review they examine Missundazstood, the No 1 album from female dance-rocker Pink.

- *Pro-Social Content: Family Portrait* finds a little girl desperate to bring peace to feuding parents ("I don't want to split the holidays/ I don't want two addresses"). *Respect* tells ladies to withhold sex from men on the prowl ("This body is a priceless piece")...
- *Objectionable Content:* They're not encouraged to abstain

entirely outside of marriage, but just not to give it away "for free." Mild profanities mar several tracks.

• *Summary/Advisory:* When focusing on social ills and family unity, Pink offers valuable insights. But her energized pop fizzles when profanity and sexual immorality take the fore.'

Plugged In understand that real dialogue flows when the young person knows that the adult is not merely highlighting the negative and has taken the trouble to do the research.

Positive Culture

It's tempting for Christians to cynically dismiss the material produced by Christian companies. Some would say that it doesn't have the production values or artistic breadth of mainstream culture. The reality, however is that Christian media companies around the world are now producing material to a high standard. They are winning respect in the mainstream arena. *Veggie Tales*, a long time staple of the Christian video market (25 million sales), has crossed over to mainstream cinema release in the United States.

Bob Walisewski (Focus on the Family), comments:

'Not only will families leave theatres giggling, they'll also be primed for some God-centred conversation about compassion, forgiveness, mercy and second chances.'

He also speaks highly of the film's artistic values:

'It's not just the exploration of biblical truth, though, that makes me a big fan of Jonah. It's also because of its snappy animation, quirky – and familiar – veggie characters, entertaining story lines and snazzy musical numbers unpredictable enough to be cool to even a few teenagers. Jonah's writing and production value stand head-and-shoulders above the crowd. For example, each and every song in this first Veggie movie easily competes with A-list Disney fare. Such professionalism deserves a lot of praise.'

The film was in the USA Top 10 at the time of writing, and seems likely to pave the way for more from the same stable.

Nor is 'crossing over' the only way that material produced by Christians will make an impact. Two mainstays of mainstream culture, *Lord of the Rings* and *Wallace and Gromit*, both reflect their creator's worldview and provide an alternative to the negative occult worldview of J. K. Rowling's *Harry Potter* or Phillip Pullman's overtly antichristian *His Dark Materials* series.

Tolkein, writing from his Catholic perspective, details a vast battle between good and evil. *Wallace and Gromit* is both whimsical and nostalgic, but it has won its committed Anglican creator Nick Park three Oscars. Its strength is not that it has a strong message, but simply that it is very funny without being offensive.

There are many others we could mention. such as the inspiring animation of *Miracle Maker*, or the massive sales of the *StoryKeepers* videos. *StoryKeepers* offers animated version of 47 key biblical incidents. The brainchild of an English vicar, they have outsold Disney video releases on occasion. The *McGee and Me* series, which examined moral themes from a Christian perspective, also crossed over into the mainstream and was screened by the BBC in a prime-time children's slot.

Churches can become ambassadors for wholesome culture by stocking books, music and videos on church bookstalls, or by promoting them from the pulpit and encouraging people to purchase them from their local Christian store.

Resource List

For further reading:
• *Children at Risk* – David Porter (Kingsway Communications)

• *A Closer Look at Harry Potter* – John Houghton (Kingsway Communications)

• *A Closer Look at Lord of the Rings* – Mark Eddy Smith (Kingsway Communications)

• *Children's Ministry Guide to Using Dance & Drama* – Ruth Alliston (Children's Ministry, Kingsway)

Your local Christian store will have hundreds of children's books and videos. You might like to check out:
• *The Oswain Tales* – John Houghton (Kingsway Communications)

Internet
• **www.family.org/pplace/pi**
A very helpful and balanced review style, which covers film, music and television. It is American orientated but provides a useful model of thoughtful reflection.

7. Tender hearted children

We will affirm and encourage those people who call out for justice, compassion and protection of children in need around the world.

At the heart of our faith is an 'other directed' impulse. Jesus was orientated to others when he gave up his life on the cross that we might know forgiveness and reconciliation with God.

Central to his teaching was the injunction to 'love your neighbour as yourself'. This was made most explicit in the parable of the sheep and the goats (Matthew 25:31-46), where he commended those who had 'fed him when he was hungry, clothed him when he was naked and visited him in prison'. The confused recipients of his blessing asked when they had done this, and he told them it was whenever they had helped those who suffered.

An 'other orientation' is a powerful counter culture response to the persistent individualism of western life, with its emphasis on personal need, personal fulfilment and personal experience.

The church and family has a three-fold responsibility in the light of Jesus' teaching and the prophetic calls of Amos, Hosea, Micah and the book of James, to avoid favouritism, act justly and trade fairly.

Firstly, we must respond to human need around the world with compassion. Secondly we must think through how we can apply these principles to our locality. Finally we must think of creative ways to pass on these values to our children.

We have a profound heritage to pass on. It has flowered throughout 2,000 years. Let us for a moment focus on the last century.

Lord Shaftesbury
Devoted his life to charitable work and social reform. Started schools in the inner city and fought hard to stop child labour exploitation.

Elizabeth Fry
A Quaker pioneer, who found herself involved in prison reform after establishing a school inside a prison.

Edward Rudolf
Founder of what is now known as The Children's Society, he started his work as a direct response to the street children he saw roaming in the area around his Lambeth Sunday school.

Thomas Barnardo
Barnardo was instrumental in helping over 60,000 children during his lifetime, and his work continues to this day. His fervour was sparked by a tour of makeshift shelters, guided by a destitute boy.

The same impulse that spurred these men and women is at work today. The gathering together of Christian agencies working with children at risk into the Viva Network is a significant spur to Christian action for the world's children. The Network's members joint budgets are thought to rival or exceed those of UNICEF.

The need being responded to is heartbreaking:

• 1.5 million children worldwide have an HIV infection.

• Over 8 million children are orphans as a result of AIDS.

• 250 million children work worldwide. Many work full time and have no schooling.

• 1.5 million children have been killed in wars during the last decade. 4 million have been injured and 12 million have lost their homes.

James echoes the book of Exodus and the words of Jesus in John 14:18, when he reminds his readers that the 'religion that God our Father accepts as pure and faultless is this: to look after orphans and widows in distress and to keep oneself from being polluted by the world (James 1:27).

There are 2.3 million local church congregations around the world. These will be the wellspring from which God's compassion will flow. What can your church do?

Think globally
Is your church involved in mission or compassion projects in other nations? Many will answer yes to this. Make a

point of researching the 'child friendly' aspects of these projects and remind both your church adults and church children of this angle.

Pass your values on

Does your church based group (and maybe even your midweek clubs and other projects) have an annual compassion project? Christian agencies can help you make connections here if none exist already. Groups such as Tearfund can provide you with material you can use with the children.

Act locally

Earlier in this book I urged you to consider doing a thorough audit of a specific area around your church. This will help you identify how many children are being reached by you and your church.

It may also help you draw together your informal knowledge about social need in the area.

Here's a snapshot of social need in a well off southern English town:

• Dozens of children exist in poverty because of the drug dependency of their parents. They need practical help with clothing and shoes and positive adult role models.

• Many single parents or families who have not lived in the area all their lives have very small social networks, and few, if any, reference points for parenting advice. Nationally and locally the social services infrastructure and health authorities are seeking out those who will offer parenting classes. They believe that the fruit will be lower health costs and a reduced need for official intervention.

• Many parents are looking for activities to do with their children; some are desperate to find safe places to spend time with them on 'access' days.

• Churches in that town are responding to this need with 'nearly new' clothes shops and outright gifts. Parenting and marriage classes will be offered by local community projects, sponsored in the main by local churches. Special parents and kids clubs provide a facility to the local community.

We must not forget
As we seek to ensure that the message of Jesus touches every aspect of the lives we are in touch with, it's vital that we put justice, compassion and social need into the filter through which we test our strategies and plans.

A strategy for children in your locality that fails to take account of social need amongst children is an incomplete one. We must have a 'no strings attached' approach to 'binding up the brokenhearted' in our communities. These are the good works that God prepared in advance for us to do (Ephesians 2:10).

If we let our lives preach then people will soon want to know what we have to say.

Resource List

For further reading:
• *Reaching Children in Need* – Patrick McDonald
(Kingsway Communications).
An excellent and resourceful overview. It has an extensive book list.

• *God's Heart for the Poor* – Philippa Stroud (Kingsway Communications).
The story of a long term care project based in a local church.

• *Miracle Children* – Duncan Dyason (Hodder & Stoughton)

• *The inspiring story of the Toy Box charity.*

Organisations
• **Viva Network**, PO Box 633, Oxford OX2 0XZ
Tel: 01865 450800
info@viva.org

• **Tear Fund**, 100 Church Road, Teddington TW11 8QE, Tel: 020 8977 9144
enquiry@tearfund.dircon.co.uk
www.tearfund.org.uk

Every Child a Chance to Choose

by Penny Frank

All children chould have the opportunity to discover Jesus and to respond to him.

- **What do children need to come to faith?**
- **How can we provide on-going training for ministers and deacons?**
- **How can co-operation across the denominations become a reality?**

Penny Frank looks at these and other critical issues for children's ministry today. Combining a positive assessment of church resources with a determined effort to trust the eternal promises of God, she holds out the prospect of a ministry that could transform our nation.

'I commend this book... I believe these pages might help us all to dig beneath our actions and feelings to ask why we are still excluding so many children from the body of Christ.'

James Jones, Bishop of Liverpool

Children's Ministry Teaching Programme

- Do you want to see children develop a personal relationship with Jesus?
- Do you want teaching sessions that are fun, biblical, evangelical and interactive?
- Would you like children to enjoy age-appropriate activities as they learn about God?

If you've said YES to any of these questions, you need the Children's Ministry Teaching Programme.

The Children's Ministry Teaching Programme provides four leader's guides covering ages from under 3 to 13+; KidZone activity sheets for children aged 5-7, 7-9 and 9-11; MiniKidz and KidZone craft books for children aged 3-5 and 5-9; a magazine for those over 11; a CD of music and stories; and FamilyZone magazine with song words, ideas for all-age worship and parents' letters.

For more information visit our website
www.childrensministry.co.uk